Contents

Flash Dash..2

Which Runner?................................8

Flash Dash..10

Translate Backpack!...................16

Translate Backpack!

Can you translate what Backpack said in the comic?

a)

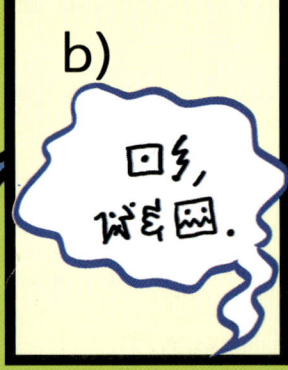
b)

c)

a) Lemonade. b) Oh, yes. c) Um ... no.